D0344489

Day By Day

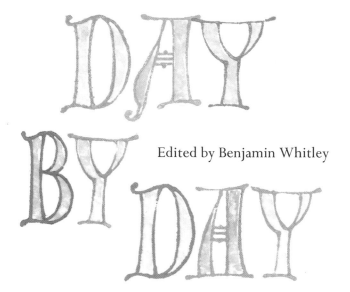

DAY BY DAY

Edited by Benjamin Whitley

Designed by Rick Cusick

Hallmark Editions

INSPIRING INSIGHTS ON MAKING THE MOST OF OUR LIVES

The publisher wishes to thank those who have given their kind permission to reprint material included in this book. Every effort has been made to give proper acknowledgments. Any omissions or errors are deeply regretted, and the publisher, upon notification, will be pleased to make necessary corrections in subsequent editions.

Acknowledgments: "Happiness Is a By-Product" from *Wild Rivers and Mountain Trails* by Don Ian Smith. Copyright© 1972 by Abingdon Press. Reprinted by permission. Excerpt taken from "Ann Landers: Let's Hear It for Us Squares" by Linda Witt from the January 1974 issue of *Today's Health*, published by the American Medical Association. Reprinted by permission of the author and Today's Health. "Recipe for Pure Enjoyment" reprinted with the permission of Farrar, Straus & Giroux, Inc. from *You Are Not the Target* by Laura Huxley. Copyright©1963 by Laura Huxley. "This Warmth of Human Relations" from *Wind, Sand and Stars* by Antoine de Saint-Exupéry, translated by Lewis Galantiere, copyright, 1939, by Antoine de Saint-Exupéry, copyright, 1967, by Lewis Galantiere. Reprinted by permission of Harcourt Brace Jovanovich, Inc. and William Heinemann Ltd., the British publishers. "Peace Within" from *Face Toward the Spring* by Faith Baldwin. Copyright 1948, 1950, 1951, 1952, 1953, 1954, ©1955, 1956 by Faith Baldwin Cuthrell. Reprinted by permission of Holt, Rinehart and Winston, Publishers. "Hour by Hour, Day by Day" from *Secrets of Self-Mastery* by Lowell Russell Ditzen. Copyright©1958 by Holt, Rinehart and Winston, Inc. Reprinted by permission of Holt, Rinehart and Winston, Publishers. "Look to This Day!" from *Look to This Day* by Wilma Dykeman. Copyright©1968 by Wilma Dykeman Stokely. Reprinted by permission of Holt, Rinehart and Winston, Publishers and Brandt & Brandt. "A Guidepost for Life" from *Another Path* by Gladys Taber. Copyright©1963 by Gladys Taber. Reprinted by permission of J. B. Lippincott Company and Brandt & Brandt. "Beware of Hopelessness" from *The Search for Serenity* by Daniel A. Sugarman and Lucy Freeman. Copyright©1970 by Daniel A. Sugarman and Lucy Freeman. Reprinted by permission of Macmillan Publishing Co., Inc. and Curtis Brown, Ltd., 60 E. 56th St., New York, N.Y. 10022. "Light in Ourselves" from *Memories of Childhood and Youth* by Albert Schweitzer. Published in the United States by Macmillan Publishing Co., Inc., 1949. Reprinted by permission of Macmillan Publishing Co., Inc., and George Allen & Unwin Ltd. "Problem Solving" reprinted with permission of Macmillan Publishing Co., Inc. from *Successful Living Day by Day* by Nelson Boswell. Copyright©1972 by Nelson Boswell. "Reflections on a Happy Life" from *Leaf & Tendril* by John Burroughs. Copyright 1908. Reprinted by permission of the publisher, Houghton Mifflin Company. "The Magic of Enthusiasm" from the book *The Tough-Minded Optimist* by Norman Vincent Peale. ©1961 by Prentice-Hall, Inc. Published by Prentice-Hall, Inc., Englewood Cliffs, New Jersey. Reprinted by permission. "Blueprint for Living" from the book *How to Live 365 Days a Year* by John A. Schindler, M.D. ©1954 by Prentice-Hall, Inc. Published by Prentice-Hall, Inc., Englewood Cliffs, New Jersey. Reprinted by permission. "It's Up to Us" from *How to Be Your Own Best Friend*, by Mildred Newman and Bernard Berkowitz. Copyright©1971 by Mildred Newman and Bernard Berkowitz. Reprinted by permission of Random House, Inc. and International Famous Agency. "One Day at a Time" by the Reverend William W. Rose, D.D. Reprinted by permission of Mrs. Mary B. Rose. "Getting the Most From Life" from *Joan Crawford: My Way of Life* by Joan Crawford. Copyright©1971 by Joan Crawford. Reprinted by permission of the publisher, Simon & Schuster, Inc. and William Morris Agency, Inc. "Your Power to Be" from *Adventures in the Art of Living* by Wilferd A. Peterson. Copyright©1968 by Wilferd A. Peterson. Reprinted by permission of the publisher, Simon & Schuster, Inc. "How's My Self-Image?" from *Creative Living for Today* by Maxwell Maltz, M.D., F.I.C.S. Copyright©1967 by Dr. Maxwell Maltz. Published by Trident Press. Reprinted by permission of Simon & Schuster, Inc. "Realizing Abilities and Facing Limitations" from *For People Under Pressure* by David Harold Fink, M.D. Copyright©1956 by David Harold Fink. Reprinted by permission of the publisher, Simon & Schuster, Inc. "Oh, the Little Daily Joys!" from *Out of My Heart* by Agnes Sligh Turnbull. Copyright©1958 by Agnes Sligh Turnbull. Reprinted by permission of Paul R. Reynolds, Inc., 12 East 41st Street, New York, N.Y. 10017. Excerpt by William Allen White reprinted by permission of Kathrine K. White, Executor of the Estate of William L. White.

©1976, Hallmark Cards, Inc., Kansas City, Missouri. Printed in the United States of America. Library of Congress Catalog Card Number: 75-13025. Standard Book Number: 87529-465-0.

Take time to play...
    it is the secret of youth.
Take time to read...
    it is the foundation of knowledge.
Take time to work...
    it is the price of success.
Take time to think...
    it is the source of power.
Take time to dream...
    it hitches the soul to the stars.
Take time to laugh...
    it is the singing that helps life's load.
Take time to love...
    it is the one sacrament of life.
Take time for friendship...
    it is the source of happiness.

Katherine Nelson Davis

TAKE TIME TO PLAY IT IS THE SECRET OF YOUTH

REFLECTIONS ON A HAPPY LIFE

The American naturalist and author John Burroughs points out that most of his happiness was unsought but came as a result of his awareness of life itself.

I have had a happy life, and there is not much of it I would change if I could live it over again. I think I was born under happy stars, and with a keen sense of wonder, which has never left me, and which only becomes jaded a little now and then, and with no exaggerated notion of my own deserts. I have shared the common lot, and have found it good enough for me....

I would gladly chant a paean for the world as I find it. What a mighty interesting place to live in! If I had my life to live over again, and had my choice of celestial abodes, I am sure I should take this planet, and I should choose these men and women for my friends and companions. This great rolling sphere with its sky, its stars, its sunrises and sunsets, and with its outlook into infinity — what could be more desirable? What more satisfying? Garlanded by the seasons, embosomed in sidereal influences, thrilling with life, with a heart of fire and a garment of azure seas, and fruitful continents — one might ransack the heavens in vain for a better or a more picturesque abode. As Emerson says, "It is well worth the heart and pith of great men to subdue and enjoy it."

O to share the great, sunny, joyous life of the

earth! to be as happy as the birds are! as contented as the cattle on the hills! as the leaves of the trees that dance and rustle in the wind! as the waters that murmur and sparkle to the sea! To be able to see that the sin and sorrow and suffering of the world are a necessary part of the natural course of things, a phase of the law of growth and development that runs through the universe, bitter in its personal application, but illuminating when we look upon life as a whole!...

All the best things of my life have come to me unsought, but I hope not unearned. That would contradict the principle of equity I have been illustrating. A man does not, in the long run, get wages he has not earned. What I mean is that most of the good things of my life — friends, travel, opportunity — have been unexpected. I do not feel that fortune has driven sharp bargains with me. I am not a disappointed man. Blessed is he who expects little, but works as if he expected much. Sufficient unto the day is the *good* thereof. I have invested myself in the present moment, in the things near at hand; in the things that all may have on equal terms. If one sets one's heart on the exceptional, the far-off — on riches, on fame, on power — the chances are he will be disappointed; he will waste his time seeking a short cut to these things. There is no short cut. For anything worth having one must pay the price, and the price is always work, patience, love, self-sacrifice — no paper currency, no promises to pay, but the gold of real service . . . .

"Serene I fold my hands and wait"; but if I have waited one day, I have hustled the next. If I have had faith that my own would come to me, I have tried to make sure that it was my own, and not that of another. Waiting with me has been mainly a cheerful acquiescence in the order of the universe as I found it — a faith in the essential veracity of things. I have waited for the sun to rise and for the seasons to come; I have waited for a chance to put in my oar. Which way do the currents of my being set? What do I love that is worthy and of good report? I will extend myself in this direction; I will annex this territory. I will not wait to see if this or that pays, if this or that notion draws the multitude. I will wait only till I can see my way clearly. In the meantime I will be clearing my eyes and training them to know the real values of life when they see them.

IT'S UP TO US

Mildred Newman and Bernard Berkowitz write of creating a rich new life for one's self in How to Be Your Own Best Friend.

You must be able to see the ways you're pulling yourself down and decide that isn't what you want to do. Then you can start doing the things that give you pride and pleasure in living....

Such as being aware of your own achievements. When you do something you are proud of, dwell on it a little, praise yourself for it, relish the experience, take it in. We're not used to doing that, for ourselves or for others. When things go wrong, they call attention to themselves. When things run well, we must actively bring them to our attention.

It is up to us to give ourselves recognition. If we wait for it to come from others, we feel resentful when it doesn't, and when it does, we may well reject it. It is not what others say to us that counts. We all love praise, but have you ever noticed how quickly the glow from a compliment wears off? When we compliment ourselves, the glow stays with us. It is still good to hear it from others, but it doesn't matter so much if we have already heard it from ourselves. This is the tragedy of some marvelous performers, who need endless applause to tell them how great they are, but who feel a chill as soon as they enter their dressing rooms. They have never heard it from themselves.

TAKE TIME
TO READ
IT IS THE
FOUNDA-
TION
OF
KNOW-
LEDGE

HOUR BY HOUR, DAY BY DAY

Why do some achieve mastery of self while others fail?
Dr. Lowell Russell Ditzen presents his inspiring views in
Secrets of Self-Mastery *and tells us a great deal about*
ourselves and the people around us.

To achieve mastery in life, we must start hour by hour, day by day, to evaluate on one side of the ledger or the other our actions in life's situations. Each time we are able to place our thoughts and behavior on the credit side, we bring more fully into existence the person who is our ideal within.

Occasionally I have time only for a hurried sandwich at a local drug store. One of the clerks is especially courteous, cheerful, and kind; his warm hello and pleasant chitchat are as nourishing to the spirit as the food is to the body. When I ask for extra mayonnaise or another glass of water, there's always prompt service, a smile, and "It's a pleasure to serve you."

Once I said to him, "I don't come in here often, but whenever I do I'm always impressed with your pleasant attitude and thoughtful service. I'm grateful for it. I want you to know it's been helpful to me, as I'm sure it is to many others. I'd like to ask, if you wouldn't mind, two questions. First, are you this way day in and day out?"

He smiled as he kept an eye on possible needs of other lunchers to the right and left. "Not always. But I keep trying. I figure most everybody is nice.

The only way to act is so they'll feel you really believe that. Now and again a customer is disappointing. But I say to myself: 'Most aren't like that.' And it's true, they aren't."

"Well, from what I've seen, you have a good batting average. The other question is this, what helps you most to keep up your good spirits?"

"Don't know, other than the thought that life's too short to mess it up with meanness and irritation. I try to remember what my dad told me: 'Son, you can be a stinker, or you can be something better.' Guess that's pretty much it: I try to be better."

If we give in to the lesser, meaner self, we not only add to the negative side of life for others. We deny ourselves a precious ingredient to good living: a feeling of self-esteem. We may not be able to control the weather or setbacks and troubles that occur in the course of a day. But we can do something about controlling ourselves. If nothing more, we will have at any day's end the second essential ingredient: self-respect.

SIMPLICITY

I know of no more encouraging fact than the un-questionable ability of man to elevate his life by a conscious endeavor. It is something to be able to paint a particular picture, or to carve a statue, and so to make a few objects beautiful; but it is far more glorious to carve and paint the very atmosphere and medium through which we look, which morally we can do. To affect the quality of the day, that is the highest of arts. Every man is tasked to make his life, even in its details, worthy of the contemplation of his most elevated and critical hour.... Simplicity, simplicity, simplicity! I say, let your affairs be as two or three, and not a hundred or a thousand; instead of a million count half a dozen, and keep your accounts on your thumbnail.

Henry David Thoreau

RECIPE FOR PURE ENJOYMENT

Here is practical wisdom for chaotic times. How to cope with a world of uncertainty is the theme of Laura Archera Huxley's You Are Not the Target. *In this excerpt we find a recipe for being a beautiful person.*

This is a recipe for beauty — *for experiencing beauty.*
    When you can do this recipe for even a few sec-onds, you will realize an extraordinary release and liberation. When you can make a practice of it, you will join a company of very advanced people. The

more artificial, hurried, and graceless your life is, the more you will benefit from this recipe.

It is a recipe for pure enjoyment....

For this recipe, choose any kind of beauty you prefer, with the provision that it be a natural beauty. Choose a beauty outside yourself, not one which may be within you, in your memory or imagination. Choose to receive five minutes of beauty through any of your senses.

To begin with, give your attention to only one sense: taste only — touch only — see only — hear only. If more than one sensation makes its way to you, do not willfully keep it out of your consciousness, but do not give it your attention either: simply let it be. Fix your attention on the one sense you have chosen.

Here are the directions:

> Choose the kind of beauty you are going to communicate with today.
>
> Cancel all thoughts from your mind.
>
> Do not name or describe or classify.
>
> Make no reference to other beauties of the past or future.
>
> Simply receive beauty, as it is.

For example, choose a taste, the taste of an apple. Bite into the apple. Taste it, without thinking about any other apple bite you have ever experienced. Simply taste the *appleness* of that apple.

Or choose to experience beauty through your sense of smell: breathe the fragrance of a flower.

Breathe it, without thinking whether it is the most fragrant, the sweetest, the best. Do not describe, compare, measure. Become absorbed in the fragrance.

Choose to see beauty. Watch a puppy's antics. Do not think of how he will look or behave when he is a grown dog. Look at him now, look at him fully, look at him so completely that there is no room in your mind for anything except this puppy, *this* moment.

> Listen to the rain — only listen.
> Listen to the wind — only listen.
> Listen to the sea — only listen.

If you choose to feel beauty through touch, only touch. Do not move your hand; only leave your hand on what you are touching — and receive.

In doing this recipe:

> *Find a comfortable position.*
> *Move as little as possible.*
> *Remain still.*

When you can do this recipe well, even for a few moments, you will experience a great sense of release from your familiar, everyday self.

This recipe is three thousand years old; it was given by Shiva to the goddess Parvati. Shiva said:

"Radiant one, see *as if for the first time* a beauteous person or an ordinary object."

As if for the first time — this is the essence.

> *It works — if you work.*

PEACE WITHIN

Where does one find inner peace? In the mountain? At the sea? Faith Baldwin, in Face Toward the Spring, *reveals a personal vision of life that comes from within.*

Nature has a way of helping us to find the peace that is always there, waiting, within each of us. My last holiday was short, but I was able to sleep in the salt air, walk in the sun, and watch the waves roll in from Spain, in a very quiet place on Cape Cod after the majority of the summer visitors had gone. This is a section I knew first in my very young childhood, again when I was in my twenties, and then did not rediscover until a few years ago. I have never been able to make up my mind in which surroundings the greatest peace is imparted to the vulnerable spirit. I have felt peace high among the mountains, and again by the sea; I have felt it on the sea in a ship, and in a Hawaiian valley. I have experienced it when the snow lay deep at the top of a ski run, and on a New England farm in autumn. I have felt it in the quiet of my own patch of land at sunup or eventide, and in the still of my own room, waking at night. I cannot truthfully say that I have ever captured it in a city street, and yet I suppose it must be there. For reason tells me that the surroundings do not as much impart as contribute, that the peace you know originates within yourself; that the setting in which you recognize it is just a key turning.

TAKE TIME TO WORK IT IS THE PRICE OF SUCCESS

YOUR POWER TO BE

Wilferd A. Peterson is a widely known philosopher and optimist. In this excerpt from Adventures in the Art of Living, *he deals with the power of* being — *the innate ability we have to be our best.*

"What you are," wrote Emerson, "thunders so loud I can't hear what you say to the contrary." You radiate what you are! You go forth to others in love, in hate, in indifference, in warmth, in coldness, in cheer or in gloom. What you truly are, deep down inside, thunders silently as you meet and mingle with people.

The greatest sculptor is not Rodin or Michelangelo. The greatest sculptor is life. You sculpture yourself into what you are by your dominant thoughts and acts. "Upon every face is written the life the man has lived," wrote Elbert Hubbard, "the prayers, the aspirations, the disappointments, all he had hoped for and was not — nothing is hidden or indeed can be."

What you are today is the result of the life you've lived up to this moment. What you will be tomorrow depends upon the quality of your life from now on. None of us is a finished product. We are each in the continual process of creating ourselves anew.

Your life emphasis should not be on possessing but on *becoming.* You should concentrate not on how you can have more, but how you can *be more.* The way in which you apply your *power to be* will determine what you *are*. Your greatest power is your *power to be*. To be more loving. To be more courageous. To be more joyous. To be more friendly. To be more sensitive. To be more aware. To be more forgiving. To be more tolerant. To be more humble. To be more patient. To be more helpful.... *To be a greater human being.*

You only achieve identity by being the best of whatever you have it in you to be, by giving full expression to your own unique spirit, to your own ideals and values, to your own gifts and talents, to your own concepts of beauty and truth.

Your power to be finds fulfillment as you relate to others. Giving of the self enlarges the self, helps you to be more. What you become, through your power to be, is mirrored in the eyes of others as the man you are. To *be more* is the supreme adventure of being.

COURAGE

In this lighthearted look at that smallest of creatures, the flea, Mark Twain presents a dramatic case for courage.

Courage is resistance to fear, mastery of fear — not absence of fear. Except a creature be part coward it is not a compliment to say it is brave; it is merely a loose misapplication of the word. Consider the flea! — incomparably the bravest of all the creatures of God, if ignorance of fear were courage. Whether you are asleep or awake he will attack you, caring nothing for the fact that in bulk and strength you are to him as are the massed armies of the earth to a sucking child; he lives both day and night and all days and nights in the very lap of peril and the immediate presence of death, and yet is no more afraid than is the man who walks the streets of a city that was threatened by an earthquake ten centuries before. When we speak of Clive, Nelson and Putnam as men who "didn't know what fear was," we ought always to add the flea — and put him at the head of the procession.

OH, THE LITTLE DAILY JOYS!

Happiness comes to us day by day. In this selection from Out of My Heart, *Agnes Sligh Turnbull suggests that time spent speculating on what might have been, or what may yet be, is time wasted.*

Even though we admit that happiness is primarily an inner condition — an attitude, if you will — the most necessary question is how one may so view the outer experience of life that this inner and most enviable state may be achieved.

My first suggestion would be to concentrate upon the small joys rather than upon the great ones. There seems to be a natural human tendency to place happiness in the future. This is, in a sense, shifting our responsibility in regard to it. We constantly say, "Oh, if I only had such a thing! If only thus and thus would happen, *then* I would be happy!" There could be no greater mistake. Unless we are happy in the present moment the chances are we will not be so in a future one. This does not mean that unusual joys when they come do not bring tremendous elation; but it does mean that unless we are in a more or less constantly happy state, the effect of large beneficences will soon fade, leaving us dependent again upon another distant hope.

But the little pleasures that daily living holds, these are the stuff by which happiness can be sustained if we only have the wit and the purpose to appreciate them. The Greeks were masters of this fine art of enjoying life. "Dear to us ever," says Homer, "is the banquet and the harp and the dance *and changes of raiment and the warm bath and love and sleep.*" The italics are mine.

Oh, the little daily joys! How precious, how satisfying they can be! The morning sunlight on the breakfast table, the smell of the air at dusk, the silly jokes, the good book, the open fire, the flowers, the sound of the clock ticking, the hour when the family come home! . . .

TAKE TIME TO THINK IT IS THE SOURCE OF POWER

LIGHT IN OURSELVES

No one should compel himself to show to others more of his inner life than he feels it natural to show. We can do no more than let others judge for themselves what we inwardly and really are, and do the same ourselves with them. The one essential thing is that we strive to have light in ourselves. Our strivings will be recognized by others, and when people have light in themselves, it will shine out from them. Then we get to know each other as we walk together in the darkness, without needing to pass our hands over each other's faces, or to intrude into each other's hearts. *Albert Schweitzer*

HOW'S MY SELF-IMAGE?

Often life leaves us with emotional scars. Dr. Maxwell Maltz, a surgeon and author of Creative Living for Today, *believes that we can draw on our inner selves to vastly heal and improve our personality.*

"While there's life, there's hope" is a saying of merit — if you feel that you deserve the good things in life, if your concept of yourself will support the idea of happiness.

Unfortunately, too many people shortchange themselves; they would never do this with money, yet they do it with thoughts. Some individuals rob themselves of everything. They worry about every minor problem . . . .

When I was younger, the intelligence quotient (IQ) was supposed to be very significant. A person would take some "intelligence" tests and receive a score. If he answered most of the questions correctly, he was labeled as a "genius" or as gifted; if he was slow or clumsy in answering the questions, he was considered subnormal or perhaps an absolute dunce.

A youngster who scored high on these IQ tests was thought of, often, as earmarked for success, while one who scored low was considered stupid — after the breadlines, then what?

I was always skeptical of the value of this IQ evaluation. My doubts have been confirmed. For years I have seen high-IQ people who have ruined their lives, low-IQ people who have lived productively.

Your self-image is so much more basic to your happiness; surely you must realize this. To me it seems obvious. If you are not only as intelligent as Albert Einstein, but also as charming as Fred Astaire and as good a golfer as Jack Nicklaus or Gary Player, you will still not enjoy life if you judge yourself critically, if you look for reasons to degrade yourself. If your self-image is weak, your positive qualities do not matter — they're irrelevant; you will find ways to torture yourself. Nothing you do will be good enough.

Therefore, when you start a day, looking for something hopeful to get you off on the right foot, don't ask, "How's my IQ today?" Instead, ask yourself, "How's my self-image? How's my S-I?" Your IQ is not important. It depends on the opinion of others. Your S-I *is* important. It depends on the opinion of yourself. Without a proper opinion of yourself, you can't function creatively.

If your S-I is all right, you can forget about your IQ and you will enjoy your day. When you walk in the street and the sun is shining, you might even find yourself whistling a tune that you love.

REALIZING ABILITIES
AND FACING LIMITATIONS

Modern life is sometimes exhausting. Its pressures are great. Dr. David Fink, in For People Under Pressure, *presents guidelines for better understanding ourselves and making our lives better and more interesting.*

This is the purpose of life: constantly to lose and recover one's balance, and by so doing to grow physically until maturity is reached and to grow mentally and spiritually as long as one lives . . . .

The more a person is able to do, the more the world expects of him . . . .

Of course no one meets every difficulty successfully. Normally, a child will persist in the face of difficulties and setbacks; that's the way all of us learned to walk. *Incidentally, by being persistent the child learns the value of persistence, which is the most important ingredient in any and all success.*

But no one can have things his own way all of the time. Situations do arise which cannot be overcome. When this happens the child says, "Well, this is too much for me; there's no use trying any more," and gives up the problem as insoluble, at least for the present. Failure after doing his best teaches him that there are some things he can't have and some things he can't do, so he restores balance by turning his attention to those more profitable directions which lead to what he can have and do.

Thus it is that he learns by experience to size up a situation and measure it in terms of his ability to manage it. Through his successes and failures he becomes a strict judge of his own worth. In this way he creates a mental picture of the world and his place in it.

Facing our abilities and limitations does not give rise to feelings of inferiority. When the baby grows up to become an eye surgeon he says that he never was any good as a gynecologist. He is covertly patting himself on the back. If he were to finish his thought, he would add, "And I'm darn glad of it because as an eye surgeon I'm tops." Similarly, a college professor is not being modest when he refuses to commit himself when questioned about things he does not fully understand. He explains, "The matter is outside my field." While admitting to ignorance he is tacitly claiming to be an authority within his own field of inquiry and in all probability he is telling the truth. The man who can say "I don't know" without the slightest embarrassment is quietly but fiercely asserting his cognizant self.

Such self-confidence is as natural as the self-confidence of a soaring bird. It's normal to have self-confidence.

BLUEPRINT FOR LIVING

Dr. John A. Schindler, in his How to Live 365 Days a Year, *suggests that we can change our way of living. And by fulfilling certain basic needs, we can really begin to live 365 days a year — and all the days thereafter.*

Handle Life This Way:

When the going is good: Tell yourself life is good, and allow yourself the delightful feeling of being happy.

When the going gets rough: 1. Stay outwardly as cheerful and as pleasant as you possibly can. Lighten an awkward situation with a lift of humor, with kindness, or a bit of a smile.

2. Avoid running your misfortune through your mind like a repeating phonograph record. Above all, do not let yourself get irritated, upset, hysterical, or self-pitying.

3. Try to turn every defeat into a moral victory....

Important Areas in Living to Watch

Keep life simple.

Avoid watching for a knock in your motor.
Like work.
Have a good hobby.
Learn to be satisfied.
Like people.
Say the cheerful, pleasant thing.
Turn the defeats of adversity into victory.
Meet your problems with decision.
Concentrate on making the present moment
    an emotional success.
Always be planning something.
Say "Nuts" to irritations.
Fill Up Your Own Unfulfilled Basic Needs

Here Is How:
If you lack love and affection from others —
*Give more than your share of love and affection to
other human beings.*
If you lack creative expression — *Go to it, nothing
is holding you.*
If you lack recognition — *Give recognition to other
people instead; some of it will come back.*
If you need new experiences — *Go and get them; be
planning something all the time.*
If you have lost your self-esteem — *Remember this:
you are just as good as I am; you and I are just as good
as they are, God bless them.*

TAKE TIME TO DREAM IT HITCHES THE SOUL TO THE STARS

LOOK TO THIS DAY!

The simple life is one of freedom and self-discovery. In her book Look to This Day, *Wilma Dykeman proposes this lifestyle as a way of being and becoming.*

Contrary to popular belief, simplicity is neither easy, common, nor inexpensive. In dress, an annual report, or a style of life, its achievement is difficult, rare, and costly in effort and taste.

Its satisfactions are unique — personal and permanent at a moment and in a world where all seems to grow increasingly impersonal and impermanent.

The simple life begins in nature and ends in human nature and seeks an elemental experience of each. It rejects the gaudy "necessities" and the trivial ornamentations by which we separate ourselves from the earth, the wind, the woods, and water, which are still man's natural habitat, despite his proliferation of concrete city canyons and labyrinths of asphalt and miasmal smogs.

It renounces the dozens of elaborate deceptions by which we separate ourselves from one another. It seeks the essential rather than the sensational in our human relationships, despite a nationally intensified appetite for the gross, the obvious, the meaningless encounter.

The simple life breaks a fresh crust of bread — and finds nourishment for the spirit.

The simple life listens to an old man's reminiscence — and touches the heart of innermost hope.

The simple life discovers a clump of fragile green ferns flourishing in a winter woods — and acknowledges the wonder of all living things.

The simple life stirs the dust of strange city streets — and recognizes a familiar face; it glimpses chaos at the heart of self-sufficiency, and plucks a festering thorn from the flesh of fleeting beauty.

Its triumph is in personal discovery of the truth that life can be found only when it is lost, that the greatness of our adventure is achieved by awareness of the small landmarks which light our daily way.

And yet — is it perhaps already as extinct as the proud passenger pigeons that once inhabited our land? Or is it simply in retreat, vanishing down the frantic highroads of power and conflict, the comfortable aisles of luxury, the congested freeways of commerce and recreation and frustration?

To pause — and look. To wait — and listen. To laugh or despair, not by proxy but for one's self — to choose. That is the freedom of the simple life, its discipline and its release. It is a way of being and becoming.

It is a freedom from self to a larger field of vision, a discipline of ideas rather than an enslavement to things, a release into that innate simplicity which is twin to the infinite complexity of the universe.

A toast! To both the sophisticated and the innocent, the believers and the doubters: Look to this day!

LIFE IS A JOY

I have never been bored an hour in my life. I get up every morning wondering what new strange glamorous thing is going to happen and it happens at fairly regular intervals. Lady Luck has been good to me and I fancy she has been good to every one. Only some people are dour, and when she gives them the come hither with her eyes, they look down or turn away and lift an eyebrow. But me, I give her the wink and away we go.   *William Allen White*

A GUIDEPOST FOR LIFE

Gladys Taber, author of the "Stillmeadow" books, speaks about the need for friends in order to make the experiment in living worthwhile.

Someone once said, "Make all the friends you can, you may need them someday." This sounds selfish to me, as does "The life you save may be your own," as if you didn't care about anybody else's life. I would say, make all the friends I can because maybe *they* might need *me* someday! And meanwhile, I do need them to make the experiment in living worthwhile.

Friendship is related to love, and if love is the bread of life, friendship is in the same package. And friendship is a very good guide. In fact, it seems to me the world situation as I write is partially due to a lack of willingness to make friends, to care about other peoples, other lands, which characterizes the rulers of many countries. If the nations could work at making friends, there would be no threat of war, ever again.

I could not rewrite history of course, but I could let friendship be a guidepost for my life.

LET'S HEAR IT FOR US SQUARES

Syndicated columnist Ann Landers is a counselor, confidante and mother figure to millions of Americans. In this selection, she proposes that the best way to get through life's problems is by means of the Puritan ethic.

...Life isn't quite as pure as the Puritan ethic would have you believe. I know because I have to deal with realities every day. There is a lot of injustice, cruelty, jealousy, destruction, hate — just a lot of things in this world that are not right. A lot of people have terrible things happen to them through no fault of their own. But in the long run, working hard and keeping your nose clean — the Puritan ethic — usually does pay off.

You see, I really am old-fashioned and square. I think there are a lot more good people in the world than bad people. I think your chances of coming out OK are better if you do what you think is right. I think that honesty is still the best policy. I think morality still pays off. I believe in all those old-fashioned things because I honestly think they work.

TAKE TIME
TO LAUGH
IT IS THE
SINGING
THAT
HELPS
LIFE'S
LOAD

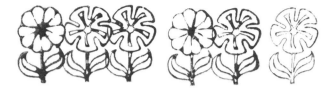

PROBLEM SOLVING

When we know who we are — and what we are — then we can find true contentment. This is the promise of Dr. Nelson Boswell in his Successful Living Day by Day.

A Four-Step Procedure in Solving Problems

There is no way to avoid problems. But the more creative we are at solving them the more effective we will be.

The better able we are to solve problems, the more we are worth to our society, our family, our organization, and ourselves. For this reason it is unfortunate that we don't spend more time learning good techniques for solving problems.

We make hundreds of decisions every day. Some are insignificant; others are vitally important. The wiser these decisions are, the more effective and happy we will be.

The rub, of course, is how to make a wise decision. One of the best ways I have seen is the following four-step procedure:

1. *Define the problem.* Perhaps the most difficult

part of solving a problem is deciding what it is. Many people waste their time because they confuse the symptoms with the problem itself. This is comparable to reducing a fever by applying cold compresses and ignoring the underlying illness. Often we don't know whether we are dealing with cause or effect. We must learn to strip away all the surrounding circumstances and define the problem precisely.

2. *Get the facts.* Benjamin Franklin used to make a list of the pros and cons of the various courses of action before he made his decision. By doing this he was able to evaluate the problem from all its aspects. And he did not have to trust his mind to keep all the facts in perspective while he reached his decision. We can't make a good decision without having all the facts.

3. *Consider the "way out" approach.* We must open our minds to all possible solutions, even though they may appear unorthodox. Inventors deal in "the unheard of approach." This is often the only way they get results.

4. *Get away from it.* Sometimes it appears we simply can't come to a decision. When this happens it is time to put the problem aside for a while. Our subconscious helps us solve many problems, and while we are relaxing the solution to our problem often pops into our mind. No one knows why the human mind works this way, but, since it does, take advantage of it.

GETTING THE MOST FROM LIFE

Joan Crawford has played many roles: wife, mother, actress, business person. In My Way of Life, *she writes of a philosophy that has enabled her to squeeze so much out of each and every day.*

People are always asking me if there's anything I regret, or would change. The answer is no! Not a thing. If I hadn't had the pain I wouldn't be me. And I like being me. Everyone should. I have a friend who says, "Treasure yourself." I follow that advice by doing a certain amount of self-pampering. I surround myself with happy colors — yellow, coral, hot pink, and Mediterranean blues and greens. I've persuaded myself that I hate things that are bad for me — fattening food, late nights, and loud and aggressive people head the list. I'm friends with myself, so I do things that are good for me, otherwise I couldn't be good for others. I spend my time with people I'm fond of, and that includes my working time, too. Whether I'm at a board meeting or on a movie set I'm with good friends, so there's no drudgery about any of my jobs.

Not that I don't work hard. The demands I make on myself are fantastic. I expect perfection. I get it, at rare moments — but they're too rare.

Probably time is my only hangup. I organize myself right down to the second because I'm greedy. Greedy to fill every minute of my days with all the things I want to accomplish. And for the future I only want a small thing: a hundred years more to act, another hundred to learn to paint, a hundred to become a writer, and still another century to get a formal education....

Squeezing the most out of life takes a little executive planning. I used to say to the children when they were growing up, "If you have twelve things to do, and twelve hours to do them in, don't spend the first ten hours doing just one thing or you'll find yourself in an awful mess at the end of the day. *Plan.* And everything will get done."

George Bernard Shaw had another way of expressing it. "If you put off your work for thirty years," he said, "then you'll have to do thirty years' work in one day — and that will be a very bloody business indeed!" And I'd like to add that you'll miss thirty years of good living!

HAPPINESS IS A BY-PRODUCT

The great outdoors offers a vastness and beauty to enhance our daily lives. This imaginative selection by Don Ian Smith, from his Wild Rivers and Mountain Trails, *gives us inspiring insight into our pursuit of happiness.*

Happiness is always a by-product of some other effort. If we seek it directly, we always miss it. But we set out after some interesting, worthwhile goal, and suddenly we realize we are happy. Filling a basket with fine trout is a challenge and an obvious goal. You use your skill, your best knowledge, your finest effort, and suddenly you realize you are having a wonderful time even if the basket is not full. Surely life is a good deal like setting out to fish on a fine fresh summer day. Our hopes are high; our goal is a basketful of fish. The day goes along. We may or may not catch the fish we hoped for. We find our plans do not always work out just as we thought they should. But with our eyes open to beauty, our ears tuned to the music of the water and the wind, surrounded with the fragrance of earth, our hearts open to the friendship of our companions, we find when evening comes we've had a very full day — even if we have an empty creel.

BEWARE OF HOPELESSNESS

Anxiety describes the era in which we live. Daniel Sugarman and Lucy Freeman, in their book The Search for Serenity, *reveal that one of the most important things we can do for ourselves is to evaluate our lives and, if necessary, change them.*

One of the most valuable things we can do to help ourselves is to look at our life, and if we find it unsatisfactory, have the courage to try to change.

The greatest enemy of change is hopelessness. When we allow ourselves to feel hopeless, we give ourselves a self-perpetuating, self-defeating mechanism which can excuse anxiety. Many distraught individuals refuse to seek help because they feel that no one could ever help them ease their suffering. Others, in treatment for a brief time, leave prematurely, diagnosing themselves as hopeless because their symptoms have not disappeared after three or four sessions.

Often the feeling of hopelessness prevents us from real self-analysis. If we resign ourselves to our fate, there is little point in attempting to find answers to the problems that plague us. We lose the desire to fathom our fantasies or to understand what a repetitive dream might be trying to tell us about ourselves. We do not want to escape from the anxiety which envelops us.

Just at the point a particular conflict may seem insoluble to both the patient and therapist, a solution may come from an unexpected source, as in the fable of two frogs caught in a bucket of cream. Both frogs made repeated but unsuccessful attempts to jump out of the bucket to safety. One frog, tired of jumping, decided not to fight any longer, and drowned in the cream. The second frog, though weary, decided he had no alternative except to continue his struggle. When he was almost totally exhausted, about to sink to the bottom, he found he was able to stand on a chunk of butter.

THE MAGIC OF ENTHUSIASM

What we so often need is a realistic approach to solving our everyday problems. Norman Vincent Peale, in a "power of positive thinking" manner, considers the impact of enthusiasm on our lives.

Enthusiasm is wonderful. It gives warmth and good feeling to all your personal relationships. Your enthusiasm becomes infectious, stimulating and attractive to others. They love you for it. They go for you, and with you, too.

People often object to this line of thought and say: But what good is there in knowing all this if you just don't happen to feel enthusiastic? You can't have enthusiasm by simply saying you have it; you don't become enthusiastic by deciding to be, just like that!

But that is just where they are wrong, very wrong. You can *make* yourself an enthusiastic person by affirming that you are just that, by thinking enthusiasm, talking enthusiasm, acting out enthusiasm. You will become enthusiastic, really so. When you associate with enthusiasm long enough it grabs you and takes over within you.

This is based on a simple psychological law. There is a deep tendency in human nature for us to become precisely what we habitually imagine ourselves as being. It is the act of image-ing or picture-ing. Hold certain images in consciousness and like a sensitive photographic film the exposure takes. We can actually become what we picture. In fact you can be dead sure that at this very moment you are what you have imaged or pictured over many years. If you are lacking in enthusiasm and happiness just take a mental rerun and add up all the dull, despondent, negative pictures of yourself which for so long a time you have fed to your sensitive consciousness which is always ready to do your bidding. Only that can come out of a person which that individual has first put into himself. When will we finally catch on to the tremendous fact that we make or break ourselves by what we do to ourselves by the images we hold?

So use this affirmation daily several times: "I think enthusiasm, picture enthusiasm, practice enthusiasm." Do this for one month, and don't weaken. If you do slip, start again at once. Keep at it and you will get the surprise of your life. And everyone around you will be astonished and pleased because you will be so very different when enthusiasm really goes to work for you.

THIS WARMTH OF HUMAN RELATIONS
Antoine de Saint-Exupéry reminds us that true happiness comes from the warmth of sharing with each other.

Life may scatter us and keep us apart; it may prevent us from thinking very often of one another; but we know that our comrades are somewhere "out there" — where, one can hardly say — silent, forgotten, but deeply faithful. And when our paths cross theirs, they greet us with such manifest joy, shake us so gaily by the shoulders! Indeed we are accustomed to waiting . . . .

We forget that there is no hope of joy except in human relations. If I summon up those memories that have left with me an enduring savor, if I draw up the balance sheet of the hours in my life that have truly counted, surely I find only those that no wealth could have procured me. True riches cannot be bought. One cannot buy the friendship of a Mermoz, of a companion to whom one is bound by ordeals in common . . . .

Happiness! It is useless to seek it elsewhere than in this warmth of human relations. Our sordid interests imprison us within their walls. Only a comrade can grasp us by the hand and haul us free . . . .

No man can draw a free breath who does not share with other men a common and disinterested ideal. Life has taught us that love does not consist in gazing at each other but in looking outward together in the same direction. There is no comradeship except through union in the same high effort. Even in our age of material well-being this must be so, else how should we explain the happiness we feel in sharing our last crust with others in the desert?

ONE DAY AT A TIME

Minister and author Dr. William Wallace Rose points out the need for facing each day as it comes and leaving the future to its own good time.

The one certain thing in this world today is the uncertainty of everything. And yet this very uncertainty which so complicates the business of living, also simplifies it. For if you . . . cannot foresee how long you are in for storm or sickness or adversity of any kind, the rational thing is to live one day at a time . . . . And that is simple. Simple, and at the same time profound. For in this manner has all the progress of the world been made.

Ernie Pyle in his *Brave Men* tells of his adventures in Italy, marching over uncertain ground in pitch darkness. After stumbling and falling several times, Pyle discovered that the soldier in front of him had a white object, a map, sticking from his pack. Pyle kept his eyes glued on that faint whiteness. When it went down, he knew a hole was ahead. When it swerved, he knew there was an obstacle of some kind to avoid. And so he kept on his feet, thinking only of the next step as indicated by the logic of events.

The person who is content to see and take the next logical move, leaving the future to its own good time, is more likely to find his way than another who throws his mind too far ahead. Don't take in too much territory at one stride. "Sufficient unto the day is the evil thereof."

TAKE TIME FOR FRIENDSHIP IT IS THE SOURCE OF HAPPINESS

Set in Perpetua, a typeface
designed by Eric Gill in 1925.
Printed on Hallmark Eggshell
Book paper.